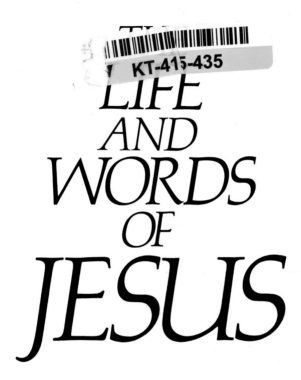

THE
LIFE
AND
WORDS
OF
JESUS

KT-415-435

A LION BOOK

Oxford · Batavia · Sydney

God's message to Mary

God sent the angel Gabriel to a town in Galilee named Nazareth. He had a message for a girl promised in marriage to a man named Joseph, who was a descendant of King David. The girl's name was Mary. The angel came to her and said, 'Peace be with you! The Lord is with you and has greatly blessed you!'

Mary was deeply troubled by the angel's message, and she wondered what his words meant. The angel said to her, 'Don't be afraid, Mary; God has been gracious to you. You will become pregnant and give birth to a son, and you will name him Jesus. He will be great and will be called the Son of the Most High God . . .'

'I am the Lord's servant,' said Mary; 'may it happen to me as you have said.'

Luke 1:26-32, 38

Modern Nazareth – a busy town as it was in the days of Jesus

No room at the inn

Joseph went from the town of Nazareth in Galilee to the town of Bethlehem in Judaea . . . to register with Mary, who was promised in marriage to him. She was pregnant, and while they were in Bethlehem, the time came for her to have her baby. She gave birth to her first son, wrapped him in strips of cloth and laid him in a manger – there was no room for them to stay in the inn.

There were some shepherds in that part of the country who were spending the night in the fields, taking care of their flocks. An angel of the Lord appeared to them, and the glory of the Lord shone over them. They were terribly afraid, but the angel said to them, 'Don't be afraid! I am here with good news for you, which will bring great joy to all the people. This very day in David's town your Saviour was born – Christ the Lord!'

Luke 2:4-11

The lights of Bethlehem shine out across the hills

The Father's only Son

The Word was in the world, and though God made the world through him, yet the world did not recognize him. He came to his own country, but his own people did not receive him. Some, however, did receive him and believed in him; so he gave them the right to become God's children. They did not become God's children by natural means, that is, by being born as the children of a human father; God himself was their Father.

The Word became a human being and, full of grace and truth, lived among us. We saw his glory, the glory which he received as the Father's only Son.

John 1:10-14

In the Temple at Jerusalem

Every year the parents of Jesus went to Jerusalem for the Passover Festival. When Jesus was twelve years old, they went to the festival as usual. When the festival was over, they started back home, but the boy Jesus stayed in Jerusalem. His parents did not know this . . .

On the third day they found him in the Temple, sitting with the Jewish teachers, listening to them and asking questions. All who heard him were amazed at his intelligent answers. His parents were astonished when they saw him, and his mother said to him, 'My son, why have you done this to us? Your father and I have been terribly worried trying to find you.'
He answered them, 'Why did you have to look for me? Didn't you know that I had to be in my Father's house?'

Luke 2:41-43, 46-49

Arched porticos in the ancient Temple area, Jerusalem

Jesus and John

John the Baptist came to the desert of Judaea and started preaching. 'Turn away from your sins,' he said, 'because the Kingdom of heaven is near!'

At that time Jesus arrived from Galilee and came to John at the Jordan to be baptized by him. But John tried to make him change his mind. 'I ought to be baptized by you,' John said, 'and yet you have come to me!'

But Jesus answered him, 'Let it be so for now. For in this way we shall do all that God requires.' So John agreed.

As soon as Jesus was baptized, he came up out of the water. Then heaven was opened to him, and he saw the Spirit of God coming down like a dove and alighting on him. Then a voice said from heaven, 'This is my own dear Son, with whom I am pleased.'

Matthew 3:1-2, 13-17

Light dances on the water of the River Jordan

Put to the test

Then the Spirit led Jesus into the desert to be tempted by the Devil. After spending forty days and nights without food, Jesus was hungry. Then the Devil came to him and said, 'If you are God's Son, order these stones to turn into bread.' But Jesus answered, 'The scripture says, "Man cannot live on bread alone, but needs every word that God speaks." '

Then the Devil took Jesus to Jerusalem, the Holy City, set him on the highest point of the Temple, and said to him, 'If you are God's Son, throw yourself down, for the scripture says, "God will give orders to his angels about you; they will hold you up with their hands, so that not even your feet will be hurt on the stones." ' Jesus answered, 'But the scripture also says, "Do not put the Lord your God to the test." '

Then the Devil took Jesus to a very high mountain and showed him all the kingdoms of the world in all their greatness. 'All this I will give you,' the Devil said, 'if you kneel down and worship me.' Then Jesus answered, 'Go away, Satan! The scripture says, "Worship the Lord your God and serve only him!" '

Matthew 4:1-11

The Judaean desert – scene of the temptation

The first miracle

There was a wedding in the town of Cana in Galilee. Jesus' mother was there, and Jesus and his disciples had also been invited to the wedding. When the wine had given out, Jesus' mother said to him, 'They have no wine left.'

'You must not tell me what to do,' Jesus replied. 'My time has not yet come.' Jesus' mother then told the servants, 'Do whatever he tells you.' . . .

Jesus said to the servants, 'Fill these jars with water.' They filled them to the brim, and then he told them,

'Now draw some water out and take it to the man in charge of the feast.' They took him the water, which now had turned into wine, and he tasted it . . . He called the bridegroom and said to him, 'Everyone else serves the best wine first, and after the guests have had plenty to drink, he serves the ordinary wine. But you have kept the best wine until now!'

Jesus performed this first miracle in Cana in Galilee; there he revealed his glory, and his disciples believed in him.

John 2:1-5, 7-11

The women come for water at Cana

No acclaim in Nazareth

Jesus . . . went back to his home town. He taught in the synagogue, and those who heard him were amazed. 'Where did he get such wisdom?' they asked. 'And what about his miracles? Isn't he the carpenter's son? Isn't Mary his mother, and aren't James, Joseph, Simon, and Judas his brothers? Aren't all his sisters living here? Where did he get all this?' And so they rejected him.

Jesus said to them, 'A prophet is respected everywhere except in his home town and by his own family.'

Because they did not have faith, he did not perform many miracles there.

Matthew 13:54-58

Donkeys line up patiently in a street in Nazareth

Follow me

Jesus went out and saw a tax collector named Levi, sitting in his office. Jesus said to him, 'Follow me.' Levi got up, left everything, and followed him.

Then Levi had a big feast in his house for Jesus, and among the guests was a large number of tax collectors and other people. Some Pharisees and some teachers of the Law who belonged to their group complained to Jesus' disciples. 'Why do you eat and drink with tax collectors and other outcasts?' they asked.

Jesus answered them, 'People who are well do not need a doctor, but only those who are sick. I have not come to call respectable people to repent, but outcasts.'

Luke 5:27-31

Teaching at Capernaum

Jesus and his disciples came to the town of Capernaum, and on the next Sabbath Jesus went to the synagogue and began to teach. The people who heard him were amazed at the way he taught, for he wasn't like the teachers of the Law; instead he taught with authority.

Just then a man with an evil spirit in him came into the synagogue and screamed, 'What do you want with us, Jesus of Nazareth? Are you here to destroy us? I know who you are – you are God's holy messenger!'

Jesus ordered the spirit, 'Be quiet, and come out of the man!'

The evil spirit shook the man hard, gave a loud scream, and came out of him. The people were all so amazed that they started saying to one another, 'What is this? Is it some kind of new teaching? This man has authority to give orders to the evil spirits, and they obey him!'

Mark 1:21-27

The impressive remains of a Capernaum synagogue built a little later than Jesus' time, show a mixture of Roman and Jewish styles of decoration

The twelve

Then Jesus went up a hill and called to himself the men he wanted. They came to him, and he chose twelve, whom he named apostles.

'I have chosen you to be with me,' he told them. 'I will also send you out to preach, and you will have authority to drive out demons.'

Mark 3:13-15

At least four of Jesus' twelve apostles worked, like these men, as fishermen on Lake Galilee

The woman at the well

In Samaria he came to a town named Sychar, which was not far from the field that Jacob had given to his son Joseph. Jacob's well was there, and Jesus, tired out by the journey, sat down by the well. It was about noon.

A Samaritan woman came to draw some water, and Jesus said to her, 'Give me a drink of water.' (His disciples had gone into town to buy food.)

The woman answered, 'You are a Jew, and I am a Samaritan – so how can you ask me for a drink?' (Jews will not use the same cups and bowls that Samaritans use.)

Jesus answered, 'If only you knew what God gives and who it is that is asking you for a drink, you would ask him, and he would give you life-giving water . . . Whoever drinks this water will be thirsty again, but whoever drinks the water that I will give him will never be thirsty again. The water that I will give him will become in him a spring which will provide him with life-giving water and give him eternal life.'

John 4:5-10, 13-14

Women draw water from an ancient well

The storm

One day, in Galilee, Jesus and his disciples set out to cross the lake: 'Suddenly a fierce storm hit the lake, and the boat was in danger of sinking. But Jesus was asleep.

'The disciples went to him and woke him up. "Save us, Lord!" they said. "We are about to die!"

' "Why are you so frightened?" Jesus answered. "How little faith you have!" Then he got up and ordered the winds and the waves to stop, and there was a great calm.

'Everyone was amazed. "What kind of man is this?" they said. "Even the winds and the waves obey him!" '

Matthew 8:24-27

Storm clouds gather over Lake Galilee

Jesus and
the children

Some people brought children to
Jesus for him to place his hands on
them, but the disciples scolded the
people. When Jesus noticed this, he
was angry and said to his disciples,
'Let the children come to me, and do
not stop them, because the Kingdom
of God belongs to such as these. I
assure you that whoever does not
receive the Kingdom of God like a
child will never enter it.' Then he
took the children in his arms, placed
his hands on each of them, and
blessed them.

Mark 10:13-16

A blind man sees

On their way to Jerusalem, Jesus and his disciples came to Jericho: 'As Jesus was leaving with his disciples and a large crowd, a blind beggar named Bartimaeus son of Timaeus was sitting by the road. When he heard that it was Jesus of Nazareth, he began to shout, "Jesus! Son of David! Take pity on me!" Many of the people scolded him and told him to be quiet. But he shouted even more loudly, "Son of David, take pity on me!"

'Jesus stopped and said, "Call him." So they called the blind man. "Cheer up!" they said. "Get up, he is calling you." He threw off his cloak, jumped up, and came to Jesus.
"What do you want me to do for you?" Jesus asked him.
"Teacher," the blind man answered, "I want to see again."
"Go," Jesus told him, "your faith has made you well."
At once he was able to see and followed Jesus on the road.'

Mark 10:46-52

A blind beggar by the Damascus Gate, Jerusalem

The dead restored to life

Jesus went to a town called Nain,
accompanied by his disciples and a
large crowd. Just as he arrived at the
gate of the town, a funeral procession
was coming out. The dead man was
the only son of a woman who was a
widow, and a large crowd from the
town was with her.

When the Lord saw her, his heart
was filled with pity for her, and he
said to her, 'Don't cry.' Then he
walked over and touched the coffin,
and the men carrying it stopped.
Jesus said, 'Young man! Get up, I tell
you!' The dead man sat up and
began to talk, and Jesus gave him
back to his mother.

Luke 7:11-15

Food for all

A large crowd came together. When the people had nothing left to eat, Jesus called the disciples to him and said, 'I feel sorry for these people, because they have been with me for three days and now have nothing to eat. If I send them home without feeding them, they will faint as they go, because some of them have come a long way.'
His disciples asked him, 'Where in this desert can anyone find enough food to feed all these people?'
'How much bread have you got?' Jesus asked. 'Seven loaves,' they answered.

He ordered the crowd to sit down on the ground. Then he took the seven loaves, gave thanks to God, broke them, and gave them to his disciples to distribute to the crowd; and the disciples did so. They also had a few small fish. Jesus gave thanks for these and told the disciples to distribute them too. Everybody ate and had enough – there were about four thousand people. Then the disciples took up seven baskets full of pieces left over.

Mark 8:1-9

A hillside overlooking Lake Galilee

Who am I?

Jesus went to the territory near the town of Caesarea Philippi, where he asked his disciples, 'Who do people say the Son of Man is?'

'Some say John the Baptist,' they answered. 'Others say Elijah, while others say Jeremiah or some other prophet.'

'What about you?' he asked them. 'Who do you say I am?'

Simon Peter answered, 'You are the Messiah, the Son of the living God.'

'Good for you, Simon son of John!' answered Jesus. 'For this truth did not come to you from any human being, but it was given to you directly by my Father in heaven.'

Matthew 16:13-17

One of the springs of the River Jordan is at Caesarea Philippi

Jesus' glory

Jesus took Peter, John, and James with him and went up a hill to pray. While he was praying, his face changed its appearance, and his clothes became dazzling white. Suddenly two men were there talking with him. They were Moses and Elijah, who appeared in heavenly glory and talked with Jesus about the way in which he would soon fulfil God's purpose by dying in Jerusalem. Peter and his companions were sound asleep, but they woke up and saw Jesus' glory and the two men who were standing with him. As the men were leaving Jesus, Peter said to him, 'Master, how good it is that we are here! We will make three tents, one for you, one for Moses, and one for Elijah.' (He did not really know what he was saying.)

While he was still speaking, a cloud appeared and covered them with its shadow; and the disciples were afraid as the cloud came over them. A voice said from the cloud, 'This is my Son, whom I have chosen – listen to him!'

Luke 9:28-35

The two sisters

Jesus . . . came to a village where a woman named Martha welcomed him in her home. She had a sister named Mary, who sat down at the feet of the Lord and listened to his teaching. Martha was upset over all the work she had to do, so she came and said, 'Lord, don't you care that my sister has left me to do all the work by myself? Tell her to come and help me!'

The Lord answered her, 'Martha, Martha! You are worried and troubled over so many things, but just one is needed. Mary has chosen the right thing, and it will not be taken away from her.'

Luke 10:38-42

Two women in a Syrian courtyard

Healing

As Jesus made his way to Jerusalem, he went along the border between Samaria and Galilee. He was going into a village when he was met by ten men suffering from a dreaded skin-disease. They stood at a distance and shouted, 'Jesus! Master! Take pity on us!'

Jesus saw them and said to them, 'Go and let the priests examine you!'

On the way they were made clean.

When one of them saw that he was healed, he came back, praising God in a loud voice. He threw himself to the ground at Jesus' feet and thanked him. The man was a Samaritan.

Jesus said, 'There were ten men who were healed; where are the other nine? Why is this foreigner the only one who came back to give thanks to God?' And Jesus said to him, 'Get up and go; your faith has made you well.'

Luke 17:11-19

This landscape in Israel is typical of the country areas in which Jesus taught and healed

The Pharisees set a trap

Some Pharisees and some members of Herod's party were sent to Jesus to trap him with questions. They came to him and said, 'Teacher, we know that you tell the truth, without worrying about what people think. You pay no attention to a man's status, but teach the truth about God's will for man. Tell us, is it against our Law to pay taxes to the Roman Emperor? Should we pay them or not?'

But Jesus saw through their trick and answered, 'Why are you trying to trap me? Bring a silver coin and let me see it.'

They brought him one, and he asked, 'Whose face and name are these?'

'The Emperor's,' they answered.

So Jesus said, 'Well, then, pay the Emperor what belongs to the Emperor, and pay God what belongs to God.'

Mark 12:13-17

A silver stater showing the head of the Emperor Augustus who ruled the Roman Empire at the time of Jesus' birth

God
bless the King

Jesus and his disciples were on their way to Jerusalem for the Passover:

'The large crowd that had come to the Passover Festival heard that Jesus was coming to Jerusalem. So they took branches of palm-trees and went out to meet him, shouting, "Praise God! God bless him who comes in the name of the Lord! God bless the King of Israel!"

'Jesus found a donkey and rode on it, just as the scripture says,
"Do not be afraid, city of Zion!
Here comes your king,
riding on a young donkey." '

John 12:12-15

A pathway leading down to the Kidron Valley, Jerusalem. A domed mosque now stands on the site of the Temple

Trouble

Jesus went to the Temple and began
to drive out all those who were
buying and selling. He overturned
the tables of the money-changers and
the stools of those who sold pigeons,
and he would not let anyone carry
anything through the temple
courtyards.

He then taught the people:
'It is written in the Scriptures that
God said, "My Temple will be called
a house of prayer for the people of all
nations." But you have turned it into
a hideout for thieves!'

The chief priests and the teachers of
the Law heard of this, so they began
looking for some way to kill Jesus.
They were afraid of him, because the
whole crowd was amazed at his
teaching.

Mark 11:15-18

A gateway in the Temple area

Betrayed!

When it was evening, Jesus came
with the twelve disciples. While they
were at the table eating, Jesus said, 'I
tell you that one of you will betray
me – one who is eating with me.'
The disciples were upset and began
to ask him, one after the other,
'Surely you don't mean me, do you?'
Jesus answered, 'It will be one of you
twelve, one who dips his bread in
the dish with me. The Son of Man
will die as the Scriptures say he will;
but how terrible for that man who
betrays the Son of Man! It would
have been better for that man if he
had never been born!'

While they were eating, Jesus took a
piece of bread, gave a prayer of
thanks, broke it, and gave it to his
disciples. 'Take it,' he said, 'this is
my body.'
Then he took a cup, gave thanks to
God, and handed it to them; and
they all drank from it. Jesus said,
'This is my blood which is poured
out for many, my blood which seals
God's covenant. I tell you, I will
never again drink this wine until the
day I drink the new wine in the
Kingdom of God.'

Mark 14:17-25

The Last Supper, remembered in bread and wine

Jesus prays

They came to a place called Gethsemane, and Jesus said to his disciples, 'Sit here while I pray.'

He took Peter, James and John with him. Distress and anguish came over him, and he said to them, 'The sorrow in my heart is so great that it almost crushes me. Stay here and keep watch.'

He went a little farther on, threw himself on the ground, and prayed that, if possible, he might not have to go through that time of suffering.

'Father,' he prayed, 'my Father! All things are possible for you. Take this cup of suffering away from me. Yet not what I want, but what you want.'

Mark 14:32-36

The gnarled bark of an ancient olive tree in the Garden of Gethsemane

Tried and condemned

Jesus was taken to the High Priest's house, where all the chief priests, the elders, and the teachers of the Law were gathering . . . The chief priests and the whole Council tried to find some evidence against Jesus in order to put him to death, but they could not find any. Many witnesses told lies against Jesus, but their stories did not agree . . .

The High Priest stood up in front of them all and questioned Jesus, 'Have you no answer to the accusation they bring against you?' But Jesus kept quiet and would not say a word.

Again the High Priest questioned him, 'Are you the Messiah, the Son of the Blessed God?' 'I am,' answered Jesus, 'and you will all see the Son of Man seated on the right of the Almighty and coming with the clouds of heaven!'

The High Priest tore his robes and said, 'We don't need any more witnesses! You heard his blasphemy. What is your decision?'
They all voted against him: he was guilty and should be put to death.

Mark 14:53, 55-56, 60-64

Death by crucifixion

They took Jesus to a place called Golgotha, which means 'The Place of the Skull.'

It was nine o'clock in the morning when they crucified him. The notice of the accusation against him said: 'The King of the Jews.' They also crucified two bandits with Jesus, one on his right and the other on his left.

At noon the whole country was covered with darkness, which lasted for three hours. At three o'clock Jesus cried out with a loud shout, *'Eloi, Eloi, lema sabachthani?'* which means, 'My God, my God, why did you abandon me?'

With a loud cry Jesus died.

The curtain hanging in the Temple was torn in two, from top to bottom. The army officer who was standing there in front of the cross saw how Jesus had died. 'This man was really the Son of God!' he said.

Mark 15:22, 25-27, 33-34, 37-39

The skull-like appearance of this rocky outcrop in Jerusalem has led some to identify it with 'Golgotha'

Alive
from the dead

Early on Sunday morning, while it was still dark, Mary Magdalene went to the tomb . . . Mary stood crying outside the tomb. While she was still crying, she bent over and looked in the tomb and saw two angels there dressed in white, sitting where the body of Jesus had been, one at the head and the other at the feet. 'Woman, why are you crying?' they asked her. She answered, 'They have taken my Lord away, and I do not know where they have put him!'

Then she turned round and saw Jesus standing there; but she did not know that it was Jesus.
'Woman, why are you crying?' Jesus asked her. 'Who is it that you are looking for?' She thought he was the gardener, so she said to him, 'If you took him away, sir, tell me where you have put him, and I will go and get him.'

Jesus said to her, 'Mary!'

She turned towards him and said in Hebrew, 'Rabboni!' (This means 'Teacher.')

John 20:1, 11-16

A first-century rock-cut tomb with a round entrance stone, at Bethphage

The meeting on the Emmaus road

On that same day two of Jesus' followers were going to a village named Emmaus, about eleven kilometres from Jerusalem, and they were talking to each other about all the things that had happened. As they talked and discussed, Jesus himself drew near and walked along with them; they saw him, but somehow did not recognize him. Jesus said to them, 'What are you talking about to each other, as you walk along?'

They stood still, with sad faces. One of them, named Cleopas, asked him, 'Are you the only visitor in Jerusalem who doesn't know the things that have been happening there these last few days?' . . .

Then Jesus said to them, 'How foolish you are, how slow you are to believe everything the prophets said! Was it not necessary for the Messiah to suffer these things and then to enter his glory?' And Jesus explained to them what was said about himself in all the Scriptures, beginning with the books of Moses and the writings of all the prophets.

Luke 24:13-18, 25-27

An ancient stepped street leading out of Jerusalem

Jesus' return

For forty days after his death Jesus appeared to his followers. They saw and spoke to him. At the end of that time he spoke about what lay ahead:

' ''When the Holy Spirit comes upon you, you will be filled with power, and you will be witnesses for me in Jerusalem, in all Judaea and Samaria, and to the ends of the earth.''

'After saying this, he was taken up to heaven as they watched him, and a cloud hid him from their sight.

'They still had their eyes fixed on the sky as he went away, when two men dressed in white suddenly stood beside them and said, ''Galileans, why are you standing there looking up at the sky? This Jesus, who was taken from you into heaven, will come back in the same way that you saw him go to heaven.'' '

Acts 1:8-11

The setting sun lights up the sky over the hills of Israel

PART TWO

WORDS OF JESUS

Good news for the poor

On the Sabbath Jesus went as usual
to the synagogue. He stood up to
read the Scriptures and was handed
the book of the prophet Isaiah. He
unrolled the scroll and found the
place where it is written,
'The Spirit of the Lord is upon me,
because he has chosen me to bring
good news to the poor.
He has sent me to proclaim liberty to
the captives
and recovery of sight to the blind;
to set free the oppressed
and announce that the time has come
when the Lord will save his people.'

Jesus rolled up the scroll, gave it back
to the attendant, and sat down. All
the people in the synagogue had
their eyes fixed on him, as he said to
them, 'This passage of scripture has
come true today, as you heard it
being read.'

Luke 4:16-21

For peasant farmers, poverty is a factor of life

Take my yoke

'Come to me', Jesus said, 'all of you who are tired from carrying heavy loads, and I will give you rest. Take my yoke and put it on you, and learn from me, because I am gentle and humble in spirit; and you will find rest. For the yoke I will give you is easy, and the load I will put on you is light.'

Matthew 11:28-30

Hear me

Anyone who comes to me and listens to my words and obeys them – I will show you what he is like. He is like a man who, in building his house, dug deep and laid the foundation on rock. The river overflowed and hit that house but could not shake it, because it was well built. But anyone

who hears my words and does not
obey them is like a man who built his
house without laying a foundation;
when the flood hit that house it fell
at once – and what a terrible crash
that was!

Luke 6:47-49

Conversation piece beneath the walls of Jerusalem

Finding life

'If anyone wants to come with me,'
Jesus said,'he must forget self, carry
his cross, and follow me. For
whoever wants to save his own life
will lose it; but whoever loses his life
for me and for the gospel will save it.
Does a person gain anything if he
wins the whole world but loses his
life? Of course not! There is nothing
he can give to regain his life.'

Mark 8:34-37

Giant poppies reach towards the sun

The bread of life

Jesus said . . . 'It is my Father who gives you the real bread from heaven. For the bread that God gives is he who comes down from heaven and gives life to the world.'

'Sir,' they asked him, 'give us this bread always.'

'I am the bread of life,' Jesus told them. 'He who comes to me will never be hungry; he who believes in me will never be thirsty . . .

'I will never turn away anyone who comes to me.'

John 6:32-35, 37

Flat loaves of bread

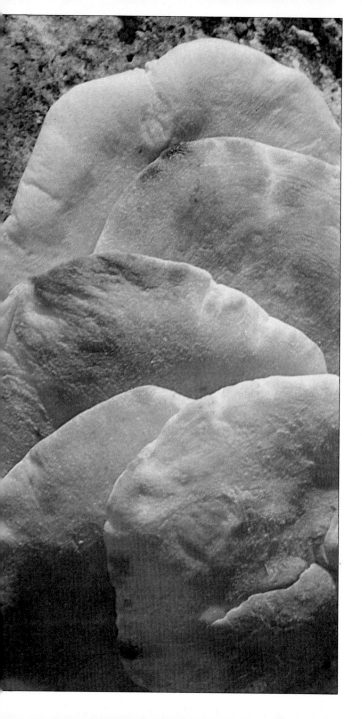

The light
of the world

'I am the light of the world,' Jesus said. 'Whoever follows me will have the light of life and will never walk in darkness.'

John 8:12

Dawn in the Dardanelles

The gate for the sheep

Jesus said again, 'I am telling you the truth: I am the gate for the sheep. All others who came before me are thieves and robbers, but the sheep did not listen to them.

'I am the gate. Whoever comes in by me will be saved; he will come in and go out and find pasture. The thief comes only in order to steal, kill, and destroy. I have come in order that you might have life – life in all its fullness.'

John 10:7-10

The shepherd's flock seek out the shade on the terraced hillsides of Israel

The way

On the evening before his death, Jesus said to his disciples: 'I am going to prepare a place for you. I would not tell you this if it were not so. And after I go and prepare a place for you, I will come back and take you to myself, so that you will be where I am. You know the way that leads to the place where I am going.'

Thomas said to him, 'Lord, we do not know where you are going; so how can we know the way to get there?'

Jesus answered him, 'I am the way, the truth, and the life; no one goes to the Father except by me.'

John 14:2-6

Stone steps mark the way in Israel

The good shepherd

I am the good shepherd, who is willing to die for the sheep. When the hired man, who is not a shepherd and does not own the sheep, sees a wolf coming, he leaves the sheep and runs away; so the wolf snatches the sheep and scatters them. The hired man runs away because he is only a hired man and does not care about the sheep.

I am the good shepherd. As the Father knows me and I know the Father, in the same way I know my sheep and they know me. And I am willing to die for them.

John 10:11-15

A shepherd with his flock amongst the olive trees in Israel

The vine

Jesus said: 'I am the real vine, and my Father is the gardener. He breaks off every branch in me that does not bear fruit, and he prunes every branch that does bear fruit, so that it will be clean and bear more fruit. You have been made clean already by the teaching I have given you. Remain united to me, and I will remain united to you. A branch cannot bear fruit by itself; it can do so only if it remains in the vine. In the same way you cannot bear fruit unless you remain in me.'

John 15:1-4

Branches are pruned to improve the yield of the vine

The resurrection and the life

Martha said to Jesus, 'If you had been here, Lord, my brother would not have died! But I know that even now God will give you whatever you ask him for.'

'Your brother will rise to life,' Jesus told her.

'I know,' she replied, 'that he will rise to life on the last day.'

Jesus said to her, 'I am the resurrection and the life. Whoever believes in me will live, even though he dies; and whoever lives and believes in me will never die. Do you believe this?'

John 11:21-26

The traditional site of Lazarus' tomb at Bethany

Hidden treasure

The Kingdom of heaven is like this. A man happens to find a treasure hidden in a field. He covers it up again, and is so happy that he goes and sells everything he has, and then goes back and buys that field.

Also, the Kingdom of heaven is like this. A man is looking for fine pearls, and when he finds one that is unusually fine, he goes and sells everything he has, and buys that pearl.

Matthew 13:44-46

A new birth

A Jewish leader called Nicodemus
came to Jesus with questions:
'I am telling you the truth,' Jesus told
him, 'no one can see the Kingdom of
God unless he is born again.'
'How can a grown man be born
again?' Nicodemus asked. 'He
certainly cannot enter his mother's
womb and be born a second time!'
'I am telling you the truth,' replied
Jesus. 'No one can enter the
Kingdom of God unless he is born of
water and the Spirit. A person is
born physically of human parents,
but he is born spiritually of the
Spirit. Do not be surprised because I
tell you that you must all be born
again . . .

'As Moses lifted up the bronze snake
on a pole in the desert, in the same
way the Son of Man must be lifted
up, so that everyone who believes in
him may have eternal life. For God
loved the world so much that he
gave his only Son, so that everyone
who believes in him may not die but
have eternal life.'

John 3:3-7, 14-17

A sparkling stream in Galilee

The people of the Kingdom

Jesus' disciples gathered round him,
and he began to teach them:
'Happy are those who know they are
spiritually poor;
the Kingdom of heaven belongs to
them!
'Happy are those who mourn;
God will comfort them!
'Happy are those who are humble;
they will receive what God has
promised!
'Happy are those whose greatest
desire is to do what God requires;
God will satisfy them fully!
'Happy are those who are merciful to
others;
God will be merciful to them!
'Happy are the pure in heart;
they will see God!
'Happy are those who work for
peace;
God will call them his children!'

Matthew 5:3-9

Love
your enemies

You have heard that it was said,
'Love your friends, hate your
enemies.' But now I tell you: love
your enemies and pray for those who
persecute you, so that you may
become the sons of your Father in
heaven.

Matthew 5:43-45

Conversation in a street in Aleppo, Syria

Don't condemn – forgive

Do not judge others, and God will not judge you;
do not condemn others, and God will not condemn you;
forgive others, and God will forgive you.
Give to others, and God will give to you.
Indeed, you will receive a full measure, a generous helping, poured into your hands – all that you can hold.
The measure you use for others is the one that God will use for you.

Luke 6:37-38

Goods are weighed and measured in the market at Bethlehem

Light for the world

'You are like light for the whole world,' Jesus said. 'A city built on a hill cannot be hidden. No one lights a lamp and puts it under a bowl; instead he puts it on the lampstand, where it gives light for everyone in the house.

'In the same way your light must shine before people, so that they will see the good things you do and praise your Father in heaven.'

Matthew 5:14-16

Oil-lamps modelled on those in use in Bible times burn with a steady flame

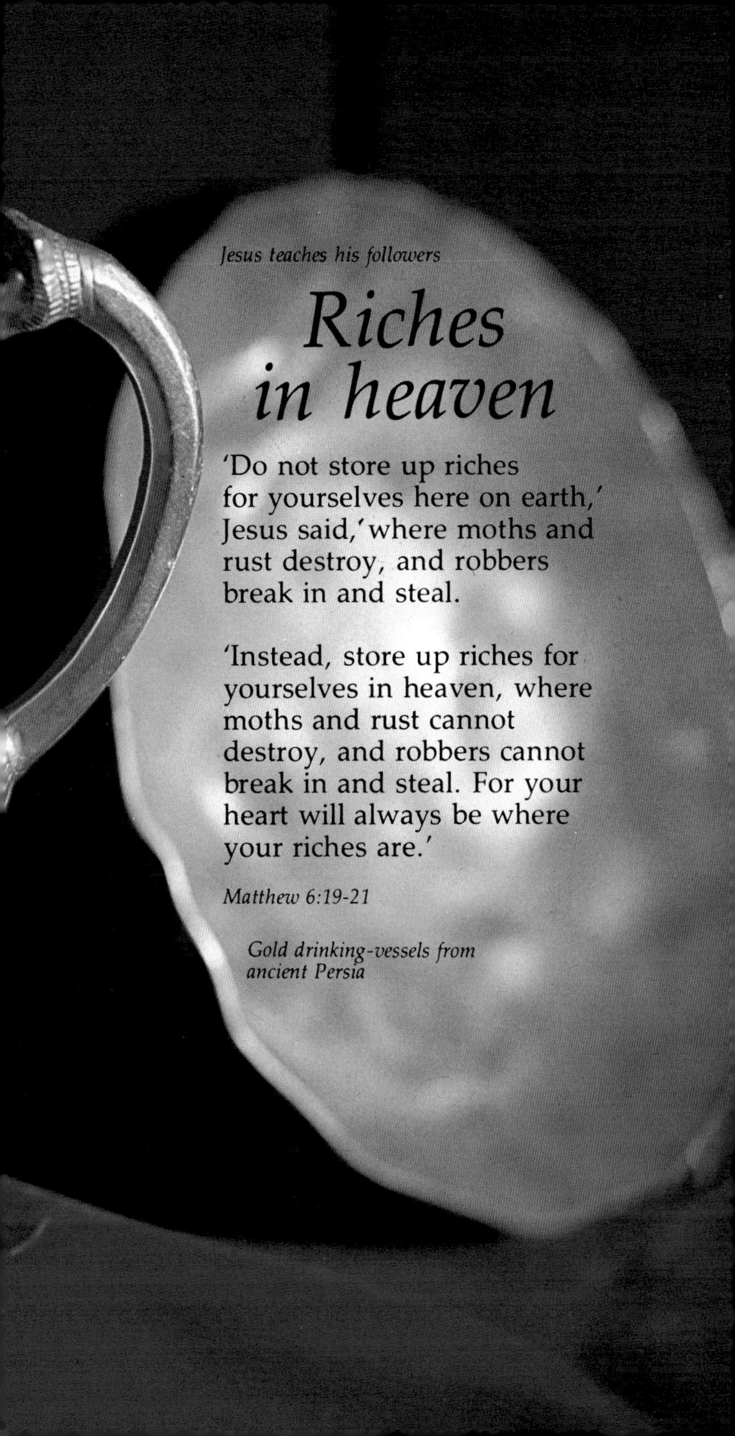

Jesus teaches his followers

Riches in heaven

'Do not store up riches for yourselves here on earth,' Jesus said, 'where moths and rust destroy, and robbers break in and steal.

'Instead, store up riches for yourselves in heaven, where moths and rust cannot destroy, and robbers cannot break in and steal. For your heart will always be where your riches are.'

Matthew 6:19-21

Gold drinking-vessels from ancient Persia

Jesus teaches his followers

A lesson in how to pray

One day Jesus was praying in a certain place. When he had finished, one of his disciples said to him, 'Lord, teach us to pray, just as John taught his disciples.'

Jesus said to them, 'When you pray,
say this:
"Father:
May your holy name be honoured;
may your Kingdom come.
Give us day by day the food we need,
Forgive us our sins, for we forgive
everyone who does us wrong.
And do not bring us to hard testing." '

Luke 11:1-4

*Ripe ears of wheat to be turned into bread for a hungry
world*

Searching
and finding

'Ask, and you will receive,' Jesus
said, 'seek, and you will find; knock,
and the door will be opened to you.
For everyone who asks will receive,
and anyone who seeks will find, and
the door will be opened to him who
knocks.

'Would any of you who are fathers
give your son a stone when he asks
for bread?
Or would you give him a snake
when he asks for a fish?
Bad as you are, you know how to
give good things to your children.
How much more, then, will your
Father in heaven give good things to
those who ask him!'

Matthew 7:7-11

*Doors to the quaint cone-shaped dwellings of Cappadocia
(Turkey)*

Serving others

Jesus said: 'The men who are considered rulers of the heathen have power over them, the leaders have complete authority. This, however, is not the way it is among you. If one of you wants to be great, he must be the servant of the rest; and if one of you wants to be first, he must be the slave of all. For even the Son of Man did not come to be served; he came to serve and to give his life to redeem many people.'

Mark 10:42-45

From ancient times to the present day donkeys have been man's beasts of burden

Love your neighbour

A teacher of the Law asked Jesus,
'Which is the greatest commandment
in the Law?'

Jesus answered, ' "Love the Lord your God with all your heart, with all your soul, and with all your mind." This is the greatest and the most important commandment. The second most important commandment is like it: "Love your neighbour as you love yourself." '

Matthew 22:35-39

Women work together to gather in the harvest

God
will provide

It is God who clothes the
wild grass – grass that is here today
and gone tomorrow, burnt up in the
oven. Won't he be all the more sure
to clothe you? How little faith you
have!
So do not start worrying: 'Where will
my food come from? or my drink ? or
my clothes?' (These are the things the
pagans are always concerned about.)
Your Father in heaven knows that
you need all these things.

Instead, be concerned above
everything else with the Kingdom of
God and with what he requires of
you, and he will provide you with all
these other things.

So do not worry about tomorrow; it
will have enough worries of its own.
There is no need to add to the
troubles each day brings.

Matthew 6:30-34

Flowers of Galilee

The promise of freedom

Jesus said to those who believed in him, 'If you obey my teaching, you are really my disciples; you will know the truth, and the truth will set you free.'

'We are the descendants of Abraham,' they answered, 'and we have never been anybody's slaves. What do you mean, then, by saying, "You will be free"?'

Jesus said to them, 'I am telling you the truth: everyone who sins is a slave of sin. A slave does not belong to a family permanently, but a son belongs there for ever. If the Son sets you free, then you will be really free.'

John 8:31-36

Eternal life

I am telling you the truth: whoever hears my words and believes in him who sent me has eternal life. He will not be judged, but has already passed from death to life.

John 5:24-25

Welcome and reward

'Whoever welcomes you,' Jesus said to his disciples, 'welcomes me; and whoever welcomes me welcomes the one who sent me. Whoever welcomes God's messenger because he is God's messenger, will share in his reward. And whoever welcomes a good man because he is good, will share in his reward.

'You can be sure that whoever gives even a drink of cold water to one of the least of these my followers because he is my follower, 'will certainly receive a reward.'

Matthew 10:40-42

A boy on a donkey passes through the Lion Gate, Jerusalem

Answered prayer

Whenever two of you on earth agree about anything you pray for, it will be done for you by my Father in heaven.

For where two or three come together in my name, I am there with them.

Matthew 18:19-20

Last promises

When I go, you will not be left all alone; I will come back to you. In a little while the world will see me no more, but you will see me; and because I live, you also will live . . .

I have told you this while I am still with you. The Helper, the Holy Spirit, whom the Father will send in my name, will teach you everything and make you remember all that I have told you.

Peace is what I leave with you; it is my own peace that I give you. I do not give it as the world does. Do not be worried and upset; do not be afraid. You heard me say to you, 'I am leaving, but I will come back to you.'

John 14:18-19, 25-28

Boats on Lake Galilee

I will be with you always

After Jesus' death and resurrection: 'The eleven disciples went to the hill in Galilee where Jesus had told them to go. When they saw him, they worshipped him, even though some of them doubted.

'Jesus drew near and said to them, "I have been given all authority in heaven and on earth. Go, then, to all peoples everywhere and make them my disciples: baptize them in the name of the Father, the Son, and the Holy Spirit, and teach them to obey everything I have commanded you. And I will be with you always, to the end of the age." '

Matthew 28:16-20

Sheep and shepherd on a coast road in Tunisia at sunset

Copyright © 1979 Lion Publishing
This combined edition © 1990 Lion Publishing

Published by
Lion Publishing plc
Sandy Lane West, Oxford, England
ISBN 0 7459 1868 9
Lion Publishing Corporation
1705 Hubbard Avenue, Batavia, Illinois 60510, USA
ISBN 0 7459 1868 9
Albatross Books Pty Ltd
PO Box 320, Sutherland, NSW 2232, Australia
ISBN 0 7324 0189 5

First edition in this format 1990

Acknowledgments
Photographs by Peter Baker Photographs: page 115; British
Museum: page 47; J. Allan Cash: pages 9, 41, 57, 109;
Stephanie Colasanti: page 26; Douglas Dickins: page 18;
Fritz Fankhauser: pages 21, 35, 45, 65, 73, 83, 85, 113,
117, 119, 121; Dave Foster: page 29; Sonia Halliday
Photographs: F.H.C. Birch, pages 3, 75, 90, 105, Sonia
Halliday, pages 49, 61, 63, 71, 79, 107, 111, 125, Sonia
Halliday/Laura Lushington, page 25, Jane Taylor, pages
31, 33, 43; Lion Publishing/David Alexander: pages 5, 7,
11, 13, 15, 17, 23, 37, 39, 51, 55, 59, 67, 77, 87, 93, 101,
103; Phil Manning: page 53; Middle East Photographic
Archive: page 89; Rex Features: pages 69, 81.

Cover photograph by Robin Bath.

Quotations from the *Good News Bible*, copyright 1966,
1971 and 1976 American Bible Society; published by the
Bible Societies/Collins.

British Library Cataloguing in Publication Data
[Bible. N.T. Gospels. *English. Today's English. Selections.
1990*] Life and words of Jesus.
ISBN 0 7459 1868 9

Printed and bound in Hong Kong